חַג הַפֶּסַח

# MY FAMILY SEDER

*by* Norma Simon

*Illustrations by*
Harvey Weiss

United Synagogue
Commission
on Jewish
Education

Copyright © 1961 by United Synagogue of America—Printed in U.S.A.
Third Printing 1976

The *Seder* night is different from all other nights.

No bread is in our house for Pesaḥ.

We eat *Matzot* at our *Seder*.

Our dinner has a special name.

Our dinner is a *Seder*.

At the *Seder*
 we read,
 we eat,
 we sing.

A *Seder* plate is in the middle of the table.

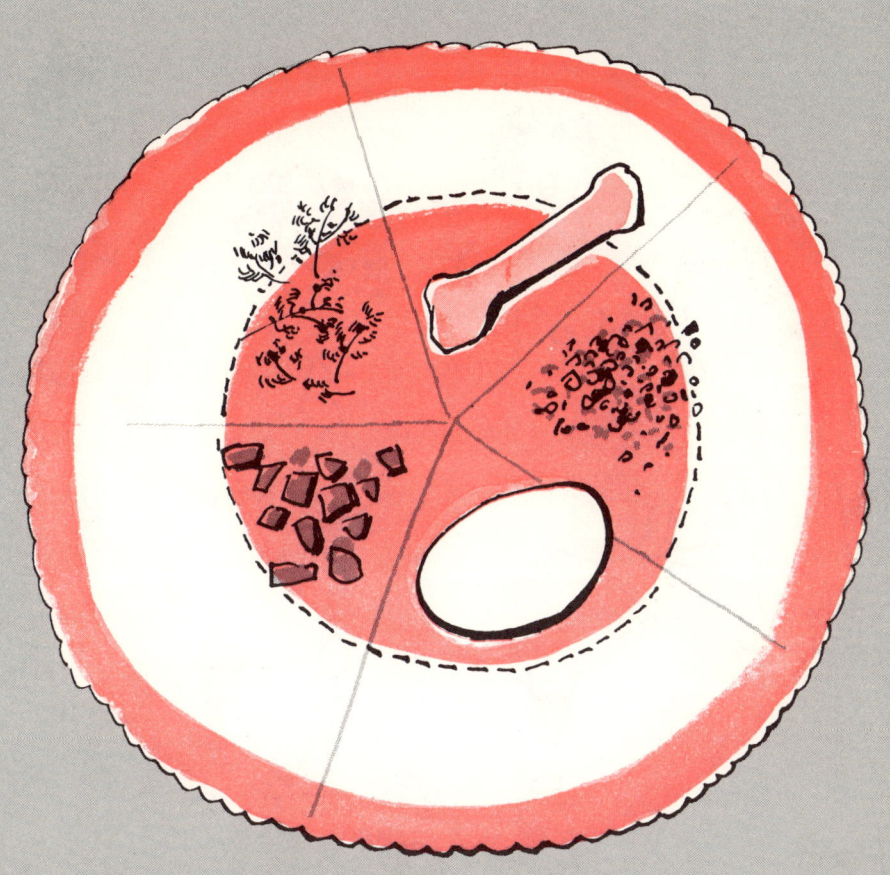

A roasted shank bone,
a roasted hard-boiled egg,
green parsley,
and brown *Haroset*,
white horseradish
are around the Pesaḥ plate.

The silver shines on the long, long table.
The glasses are filled with Pesah wine.

My Grandpa, my Grandma, my uncles,
my aunts, and all my cousins,
Susan, Amy,
Nancy and Nathan,
all come to the *Seder*.

My Grandpa sits on pillows.
His chair becomes a soft, white throne.

Near my Grandpa,
>   in a soft, satin cover,
>   are the three *Seder Matzot*.

The *Matzot* are near Grandpa because
>   he leads the *Seder*.

Every year,    every Pesaḥ,
>   Grandpa leads the *Seder*.

Every year,     every Pesaḥ,
    David and I    and all my cousins,
    wait    and    wait,
    wait    and    wait,
until the candles are burning,
until the *Kiddush* is said,
until the wine is tasted.

Grandpa takes the middle *Matzah*
>out of the satin cover.

He breaks the *Matzah* down the middle.

Now there are two halves.

One half stays in the satin cover.

One half goes under the soft, white pillows.

The *Matzah* under the pillows is the *Afikomen*.

This *Matzah* is special
>to the children at the *Seder*.

Cousin Nathan asks the Four Questions.

Grandpa and Daddy and my uncles,
Grandma and Mother and my aunts
    read the *Hagadah*,
        the book that tells the story of Pesaḥ.
Uncle Judah sits near the children.
He tells us the story.

Every year,     every *Pesaḥ*,
    Uncle Judah tells us the story,
    about Moses and Miriam,
    about the Princess and the Pharaoh,
    about Egypt long ago.

**W**e wait and wait
    and wait and wait
    until Grandpa and Daddy
    and all the uncles
    go out to wash their hands.
The minute they are gone,
    we take the *Afikomen!*

Susan says,   "Hide it in the bookcase!"
Amy says,     "Hide it under the couch!"
David says,   "The bedroom!"
Nancy says,   "The kitchen!"
I say,        "Hurry, hurry, hurry, here they come!"

Grandpa, Daddy, and all my uncles
 come back to the table.
The *Afikomen* is gone,
 but they don't know it.
All my cousins,
 and David and I,
 giggle to each other.

Every year,    every Pesaḥ,
> we hide the *Afikomen*.

Then we wait again,
> and wait  and wait  and wait.

Grandpa and Daddy and all my uncles,
Grandma and Mother and all my aunts
> read more in the *Hagadah*.

We eat the Pesaḥ dinner
> my grandma and my mother cooked.

Then Grandpa says,
> "Where's the *Afikomen*?
> We have to have the *Afikomen!*
> Has anyone seen the *Afikomen*?"

He asks my mother,
> "Miriam, did you see the *Afikomen*?"

He asks my father,
> "Jonathan, did you see the *Afikomen*?"

Every year,    every Pesaḥ,
  Grandpa looks for the *Afikomen*.
Susan laughs,
   "I know where it is, Grandpa."
Amy laughs,
   "I know where it is, Grandpa."
Nancy laughs,

   "I know where it is, Grandpa."
David laughs,
   "I know where it is, Grandpa."
All the cousins laugh,
   and I laugh,
   "We know, Grandpa."

Grandpa looks surprised and says,
"Where is it, then?"
He promises a present,
one for every child.
Every year,    every Pesaḥ,
Grandpa promises a present,
one for every child,
and we give back the *Afikomen*.

We run into the kitchen,
> open up the closet,
>> take out the *Afikomen*,
>>> and bring it back to Grandpa.
Grandpa smiles a very big smile.
He pats us all on the head.

We drink more wine;
 our singing is happy.
The night is long
 and we all grow sleepy.

My cousins and David wait with me
for the *Ḥad Gadya,*
and the good-byes at the door.

When my light is out,
    and my eyes begin to close,
   I like to sing to myself.

Da - da - ye-nu, ⎯ da - da - ye-nu, ⎯
da - da - ye - nu · da - ye-nu, da - ye-nu, da - ye-nu.
Da - da - ye-nu, ⎯ da - da - ye - nu, ⎯
da - da - ye-nu, da - ye-nu, da - ye-nu.

Every year, every Pesaḥ,
   I sing myself to sleep.

## WORDS FOR PRONUNCIATION AND DEFINITION

*Seder* (SAY-der) — Passover home service on first and second nights of the festival.

Pesaḥ (PAY-saḥ) — Passover.

Four Questions — The *Seder* is initiated by a young child asking four questions about the Passover.

*Matzot* (Mah-TZOT) — Unleavened bread eaten on the Passover.

Pesaḥ plate — A large plate on which the Passover symbols are arranged.

*Afikomen* (Ah-fee-KO-man) — A piece of *Matzah* hidden at the beginning of the *Seder*, to be eaten at the end of the Passover meal.

*Kiddush* (Kid-DOOSH) — A blessing over the wine.

*Hagadah* (Hah-gahd-DAH) — The book from which the *Seder* service is read.

*Had Gadya* (Had Gahd-YAH) — A children's song sung at the end of the *Seder* service.

*Da-da-ye-nu* (Dah-dah-YĀ-noo) — A *Seder* hymn.